8/13

W9-AXY-813

WITHDRAWN

Xtreme Athletes

Brock Lesnar

Xtreme Athletes

Brock Lesnar

Jeff Savage

MORGAN REYNOLDS
PUBLISHING

Greensboro, North Carolina

Xtreme Athletes

Brock Lesnar
Apolo Ohno
Tito Ortiz
Danica Patrick
Michael Phelps
Kelly Slater
Michelle Wie
Shaun White

Xtreme Athletes: Brock Lesnar

J-B
LESNAR
420-3967

Library of Congress Cataloging-in-Publication Data

Savage, Jeff.
 Brock Lesnar / by Jeff Savage.
    p. cm. -- (Xtreme athletes)
 Includes bibliographical references and index.
 ISBN 978-1-59935-185-8 (alk. paper) -- ISBN 978-1-59935-211-4
(e-book :
alk. paper) 1. Lesnar, Brock. 2. Wrestlers--United States--Biography.
I.
Title.
 GV1196.L47S28 2012
 796.812092--dc23
 [B]

                                    2011024365

*For George Macchia—whose friendship matches
the strength of a hundred Brock Lesnars*

Contents

Lesnar, top, in action against an opponent during a UFC bout

one
Life on a Farm

Brock Lesnar was in a rage as he slammed Frank Mir to the ground. The crowd at the Mandalay Bay Events Center in Las Vegas gasped in awe. Brock was the barrel-chested giant who out-muscled mixed martial arts opponents with frantic violence in the Octagon. In this 2009 Ultimate Fighting Championship (UFC) heavyweight title fight, Brock bulldozed Mir into the cage and controlled him in a side mount. He pounded Mir's face with his huge fists until the referee stopped the fight. In the most-watched TV pay-per-view event in history, fans saw why Brock was being called "The Baddest Dude on the Planet." Such a beating was nothing new to Brock. He was built for destruction from the start.

Brock Edward Lesnar was born July 12, 1977, in Webster, South Dakota. He weighed nine pounds, nine ounces at birth. His nickname was Pork Chops growing up on a dairy farm with his parents, two older brothers, and younger sister. The Lesnars had about two hundred cows but always seemed to struggle to make ends meet. John Schiley, the Webster High School wrestling coach, said, "They never had the capital or equity enough to get 'em going. And every day was a day to try to buy milk and keep the family fed."

Brock worked hard on his farm, milking cows, shoveling manure, and hauling bales of hay. By age five he suffered two hernias lifting hay bales. Brock says it was on his farm that he developed a strong work ethic. "I don't (complain). That's the way I was brought up," Brock says. "I learned important lessons on the farm. I couldn't do anything until my work was done."

Brock was like most boys growing up in Webster in many ways. He got his first gun, a Crosman air rifle, when he was six years old. "I pretty much tried to clean out the blackbird population on the farm," Brock said. One of Brock's biggest joys was sleeping in the hay loft in the barn.

Brock was raised on a dairy farm.

He treated it like a jungle gym, swinging from the crossbeam and jumping to the ground. He did push-ups, sit-ups, and pull-ups for as long as he could because he wanted to grow stronger.

"From a really young age, I was a physical kid who enjoyed physical contact," Brock said. "My older brothers fought a lot. It was just part of living in a small town, I guess. It was one of those things to do on the weekend. I was always scrapping."

Brock says that growing up on the farm surrounded by nature is what shaped him; that his desire to fight comes naturally. "Let's say you have a bird feeder out, and you watch these squirrels and birds: They fight over food. That's the way it is," Brock explains. "We tend to forget exactly who we are and what we're about. Fighting's been around since the first day of life."

Brock's oldest brother, Troy, is eight years older. Chad is six years older. Brock watched Troy and Chad play competitive sports like football and wrestling. Later, Brock's younger sister, Brandy, would play sports, too. Brock was eager to wear a uniform and play competitively. His sport would be wrestling, and he started when he was five years old. When Brock was older, he realized he was lucky. A lot of his friends weren't allowed to play sports or be involved in any other after-school activities. Afternoons were spent doing farm chores, and there was little time for anything else. But Brock's parents wanted to instill in their son a sense of triumph.

Brock remembers sitting in the back of the family station wagon riding past endless farm fields on his way to yet another wrestling tournament. His mother was usually the one driving. His father mostly stayed home to work the farm. His mother, Stephanie, was hard on Brock. She expected him to win. When he lost, which sometimes happened, she would say, "Admit it, accept it, get in the car, and let's go home." Brock would feel awful on the ride home, and he remembers his mother telling him the same thing, "There's another match next weekend. If you don't like the way you feel when you lose, then get in there and win. What do you want to be in life? The guy who feels good because he wins, or the guy who feels like you do now because he lost?"

Fortunately, Brock won most of his matches. When he did win, his mother would say, "Good job, Brock. You won. That's what you're supposed to do." Upon his return home, Brock would receive similar treatment from his father.

Brock's parents made it clear that winning was the natural order of things. They taught him to never settle for anything less. Some boys would have withered in the face of such pressure. But Brock accepted the challenge. "At a very young age I developed an inner confidence that I still have today," he says. "I don't know if it's ego, attitude, arrogance, or something else. But whatever it is, it works for me."

Brock was allowed to join the Webster High School wrestling team as a seventh-grader. The first thing coach John Schiley noticed about Brock was his appetite. Brock sometimes worked on Schiley's farm, and he would sit down with the family for lunch. "He was always a big eater, always loved milk," Schiley said. "There was a roast for Brock, a gallon of milk for Brock, and a roast and a gallon of milk for the rest of us."

High school wrestlers

Naturally, Brock grew fast. He started the season wrestling at 103 pounds. On January 4, 1991, wrestling at 119 pounds, Brock won a 12-6 decision over Greg Holland to help Webster beat Roncalli High. Later that month, he pinned Cory Bremmon to lead Webster past Britton High. On February 3, Brock moved up to the 125-pound class to wrestle a senior and was pinned. It was his last varsity match of the season. The coach didn't want to burn him out to early.

The following year, Brock wrestled at 125 and 130 pounds and enjoyed moderate success. As a ninth-grader, he truly blossomed. He started the season weighing 143 pounds, yet he wrestled in the heavier 152-pound class. It was a challenge to compete against opponents nine pounds heavier, but Brock knew it would make him better. He pinned his first opponent of the season just 1:49 into the match to lead the Bearcats to a win over Deuel High. Coach Schiley said of Brock, "I wondered if he should have been wrestling in that weight class. I was impressed by him."

Brock had a mix of wins and losses against older opponents, and after a particularly successful tournament late in the season, Schiley told a local newspaper, "Brock had his best tourney yet. I'd consider a freshman at 152 pounds a success because he's

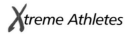

usually wrestling juniors and seniors. He's the most improved wrestler on the team at this point." Brock finished the regular season with a record of 18-13. In the district tournament, he beat Wade Brendan, 6-5, to advance to the 152-pound championship match. His opponent was Darin Anderson, a strong wrestler who had pinned Brock in less than a minute in the first week of the season. This time, Brock pinned Anderson. Brock completed his freshman season by finishing second in the regional meet.

Brock continued to work hard on his family farm. As he did his chores, he daydreamed about wrestling. He wanted to get stronger, but he had no money to buy weights. So he made his own gym equipment. He built a bench from scrap wood to perform bench presses. Sometimes he bench-pressed from the ground. He lifted rocks. He lifted a fifty-five gallon drum. He lifted farm equipment. Through sheer determination and sweat, he transformed his lanky frame into a body packed with muscles.

As a sophomore, Brock played on the school's football team as a lineman, mainly to be with his friends. His sport was wrestling, and he competed that year in the 160-pound class. He was growing fast and would eventually compete in the heavyweight class, but in the meantime he capitalized on being at the lower weight classes. "I developed the moves and quickness of a lighter-weight wrestler," he said. "When I got to heavyweight, I still had those moves, and I was fast. Had I always been big, I probably would have skated by on strength and size alone, and I never would have learned to move like I do now."

Brock's sophomore season was a success as he helped the Bearcats to a second-place finish at the South Dakota state meet. His favorite matches were his victories over several wrestlers who had beaten him the year before. Revenge felt sweet to Brock.

Brock dominated his junior year on the football field. He was a two-way starter on the line. As a nose guard on defense, he was double-teamed on every play. Still, he led the team with twelve tackles in a 23-0 win over Redfield High. He had eleven tackles in a 16-6 win over Milbank High. He led the Bearcats once more with nine tackles in a 21-13 loss to Clark High. Football was fun for Brock, but really, he was just waiting for the wrestling season.

This season began with disappointment. In the opening team victory over Deuel High, Brock lost to Jason Bauman, 7-1. Brock was frustrated. He was wrestling at 189 pounds now. He knew he was quicker than his opponents. With all of the strength training he was doing on his farm, he certainly was stronger. By now, he could deadlift nearly six hundred pounds. He expected more from himself than a loss in a regular meet.

At his next competition in a five-team tournament, Brock swept the field, going 4-0, with three pins. In the next tournament five days later, he went 3-0. Later in the season he pinned six straight opponents. He finished the regular season with a 33-3 record.

In the state meet, he opened with an 11-0 victory. He had visions of being the state champion but was defeated in the quarterfinals of the South Dakota state wrestling tournament by Eric Porisch, 6-3. In the wrestlebacks (losers bracket), Brock won three straight matches, two by pins, to earn the chance to finish in third place. His opponent in the third-place match was Porisch again. Brock craved revenge. He dominated Porisch to win, 8-2, and took third place in the state. Brock wasn't satisfied with that.

During Brock's junior year, a recruiter for the National Guard showed up at Webster High. Brock knew for some time he wanted to find a way off the family farm. Here was the way, he thought. He signed up for the Guard and got his mother to cosign for him.

When summer came, Brock was shipped to Fort Leonardwood, Missouri. The nine weeks he spent with the National Guard changed his life. "I was 17 years old, a typical teenager," he said. "I didn't listen to many people. I was Mr. Know-It-All. I didn't respect myself or authority. Then I entered the Guard. Those [guys] straightened [me] out right away."

Brock and the rest of the troops had to be up by dawn and on the move. Each day started with a run to build endurance. In a few weeks, Brock improved his speed to the point that he ran the two-mile distance in 10:56.

Brock intended to stay in the Guard. He was assigned to the artillery supply unit. The explosive charges were coded red and green and an eye exam

The National Guard logo

revealed Brock to be red-green color-blind, and he was reassigned as a clerk. When he could not pass the typing test he was sent home to Webster. "Lucky for me," Brock says now.

Someone who is red-green color-blind will see the bottom colorway. A person without vision deficiencies sees the top image.

Brock resumed high school life as a senior. The football team started the season with three straight losses, so the coach made a drastic decision. He put the team's toughest player—Brock Lesnar—in the backfield. The plan was to give Brock the ball and see if the other team could stop him.

Webster's next game was homecoming against Redfield High. Play after play, Brock took the handoff up the middle and plowed into the defense. He scored the game's first touchdown. He scored the next touchdown, too. By halftime, Webster led, 35-0. Brock finished with 113 yards rushing in a 50-0 victory.

The following week against Milbank High, Brock carried twelve times for ninety-two yards and scored the team's only touchdown in a 14-9 loss. One week later against Roncalli High, Brock was leading his team again. In the third quarter, he had already rushed thirteen times for fifty-three yards

Brock proved his toughness and agility on his high school's football team.

and caught two passes for twenty-eight more. Then disaster struck. Brock was an upright runner, and he stood too high when a defensive back drilled him. He collapsed in pain. He had suffered a serious knee injury.

The injury required surgery, and Brock needed eight weeks to recover. Wrestling season starts immediately after football ends, and Brock was obsessed with being ready in time. On the first day of practice, the wrestlers were required to do a six-mile run called "gut check" in order to make the team. Brock was on crutches. Coach Schiley told Brock that he certainly did not need to do the run. But Brock knew he was the team's leader and that the underclassmen looked up to him. He did the run on crutches, hobbling along the road, with the coach following behind in his pickup. Finally the coach told Brock he had made his point and to climb in the back of the pickup.

When the matches began, Brock was ready. He pinned his first opponent in eighteen seconds. At the five-team Watertown Tournament, he pinned all four of his opponents. He started the season with nine straight pins. Brock wasn't just winning; he was crushing his opponents. He weighed 210 pounds now, and he bulldozed his way to a 30-2 regular-season mark.

At the South Dakota state tournament, he finished third again, getting outpointed, 4-1, by Brian

Van Emmerik in the semifinal round. It was a bitter loss for Brock. No colleges had offered him a wrestling scholarship, largely due to his poor grades. Of the fifty-four seniors in his 1996 graduating class, he finished last academically. He had hoped that winning the state title would maybe attract some interest from college recruiters. When it did not happen, Brock was faced with a choice: attend a community college or work the family farm. Brock chose community college.

Brock, right, defeated Iowa's Wes Hand, left, during the NCAA Division I Wrestling Championships held in St. Louis, Missouri, on March 18, 2000.

two
College
Champion

L esnar packed up his belongings in his Monte Carlo sedan and drove north to Bismarck, North Dakota. Mike Wiley, an assistant wrestling coach at Bismarck State Junior College, had convinced Lesnar to join his wrestling program. Wiley was a Webster High graduate who had seen Lesnar wrestle. He knew Lesnar could be great.

Lesnar moved into the basement of school athletic director Ed Kringstad's house. As a freshman, Lesnar blew through the competition to compile an 18-2 record. Then came the National Junior College Athletic Association (NJCAA) national championships. Lesnar expected nothing less than first place.

In the first round, he beat Tim Ellis of Harper-Illinois College, 7-0. In the second round, he scored a takedown with fourteen seconds left in the third period to pull out a 3-2 victory over Gordon Campbell of Muskegon-Michigan College. But in the quarterfinals, Lesnar was stunned, 5-4, by Damion Martindale of Clackamas-Oregon College. "The loss to that pudgy no-name was a major turning point in my life," Lesnar said. "There was no way that kid should have been able to beat me. At that moment I looked inside myself, and I got serious. I vowed to be the biggest, strongest, fastest, meanest SOB I could become."

Lesnar had gained twenty pounds during his freshman year at Bismarck. As a sophomore, he gained twenty more. He worked hard in the weight room to pack on muscle. Soon he was up to 250 pounds. That year, he tore through opponents with brute force. After he ran his record to 22-0 he told the _Bismarck Tribune_ that he had one goal. "I'm going to win it," Lesnar said. "I'm going to be a national champion this year. I've been wrestling too long and working too hard to let this one go."

Lesnar entered the NJCAA national meet with a 29-0 record and ranked No. 1 in the country. He pinned his first opponent in twenty-four seconds. He pinned his next opponent in 1:37. He beat his semifinal round opponent by a 3-1 score.

He met Dave Anderton of Ricks, Idaho, in the title match. Anderton had beaten Lesnar twice the year before. "Those are the kind of things that just burn in you," Lesnar said. Lesnar took a commanding 5-0 lead on Anderton this time, but Anderton recovered in the second round to tie it, 6-6. Both wrestlers scored reversals to end the round at 8-8. In the dying seconds of the final round, Anderton scored a point on an escape to take a 9-8 lead. Lesnar was desperate. He responded with a takedown for two points and a 10-9 lead. He held on for the final thirteen seconds and scored one more point for riding time in an 11-9 victory. He was national champion. In a strange twist, Lesnar was the last person ever to wrestle for Bismarck Community College. After his victory, the school dropped the wrestling program due to a lack of funding.

As Lesnar was steamrolling opponents his sophomore season, top-notch Division I-A colleges took notice. At the Bison Open in Fargo, North Dakota, wrestlers from all college levels were there, including standouts from wrestling powerhouse University of Minnesota.

When Gophers wrestling coach J. Robinson saw Lesnar blow through the competition to win the heavyweight class, he approached Lesnar. "I asked him if he was looking to wrestle in college, and he said yes," Robinson recalled. "I asked him if he'd be interested in coming down on a visit, and he said yes."

Lesnar went to the University of Minnesota on a recruiting trip. The next day, he signed a letter of intent to attend Minnesota. Now that Lesnar's season at Bismarck was over, he was on his way to Minneapolis to train with the Gophers.

The University of Minnesota welcome sign

Lesnar moved into a dusty attic in a fraternity house and worked for a construction company demolishing things with a sledgehammer. He lifted weights and practiced wrestling moves with his teammates in the afternoon.

The fall season was still three months away, but Lesnar was learning important techniques. Coach Robinson called Lesnar into his office one day. There was a problem. Lesnar was not eligible yet to transfer to the University of Minnesota. He needed twenty-four more credits worth of classes, which meant he needed to attend summer school. Unfortunately, the community colleges in the area had just started their summer classes. Robinson made some calls. The next thing Lesnar knew, he was driving his old Mazda RX-7 to California.

He arrived at Lassen Community College in Susanville the morning of his first day of classes. He barely had enough money to pay for rent and school cafeteria meals and had to borrow textbooks from schoolmates. Lesnar focused on his studies and gained a full course load of sixteen credits, and returned to the Midwest. He needed eight more credits. He went back to Bismarck College in the fall and took classes worth twelve credits, just to be safe. He enrolled at the University of Minnesota just in time for wrestling season.

Lesnar moved in with teammates Tim Hartung and Chad Kraft. He was in the best shape of his life and told everyone he intended on being the NCAA Division I heavyweight champion.

Then, in his first competition as a Gopher, he was humbled. At the Great Plains Open in Lincoln,

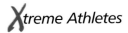

Nebraska, Lesnar won his first three matches. He expected to win his weight class. Instead, he lost to Iowa State's Trent Hynek, 5-3.

Lesnar was embarrassed. Here he was, bragging to everyone who would listen, that he was going to be the best heavyweight in the country, and he lost in his first tournament. He summoned a deeper inner force that had begun to define him, and he never lost—until his last match of the season.

In between, Lesnar was everything the Gophers had hoped for. He stunned Iowa superstar Wes Hand to move up to No. 2 in the national rankings. He won Big Ten Wrestler of the Week honors. He beat Hand again to help end Iowa's streak of twenty-five straight Big Ten Championships. He led the Gophers to their first Big Ten Championship in fifty years.

At the national championships at Penn State University, the meet wasn't decided until the last match. The Gophers could win their first-ever NCAA wrestling title if Lesnar could win his final contest. It was a match to decide the national heavyweight champion.

Lesnar was matched against defending national champion Stephen Neal from Cal State Bakersfield. Neal hadn't lost a match in two years. He would later win a world wrestling championship and two Super Bowl rings as a lineman for the New England Patriots.

Cal State Bakersfield's Stephen Neal, left,
defeated Lesnar for the championship title.

Lesnar did all he could against Neal. In the end, he barely lost, 3-2. People heaped congratulations on him for making it to the finals and Lesnar tried to act gracious. Inside, he seethed. Being the NCAA Division I runner-up was unacceptable to him. "I am either number one, or I am a loser," Lesnar said years later. "I hated losing to Neal. I had one more year to make my dreams come true, and at that moment I made up my mind that I was going all the way. There wasn't a college wrestler on the planet who was going to stop me."

By his own admission, Lesnar was obsessed. He devoted every thought and action he could toward winning the 2000 NCAA title. He came out blazing and never let up. He tossed opponents across the mat with such force that Gophers matches became a true spectacle in the Twin Cities area.

The Minnesota wrestling program seized on its moment in the spotlight. Fans attending the meets were given posters of Lesnar titled "Brockfast of Champions" that showed Lesnar's neck and biceps measurements. Newspaper reporters interviewed him constantly, and he became a regular guest on KFAN-radio's weekly wrestling program.

Before long the attention overwhelmed Lesnar. He just wanted to wrestle and told his coaches that he no longer wanted to talk to the media. Assistant coach Marty Morgan explained to Lesnar that it was good for the program for him to talk to reporters, and Lesnar understood.

Lesnar's record was 22-0 when Minnesota, ranked No. 2 in the country, met top-ranked Iowa in the regular season finale. A crowd of 13,128 filled Williams Arena—the largest ever to see a wrestling event. Lesnar met rival Wes Hand, and he lost, 5-4. Lesnar was angry. That night, he couldn't even eat his dinner. But he tried to keep the loss in perspective. After all, this wasn't the match that mattered most, he told himself. "Better to lose now than then," he said.

Two weeks later at the Big Ten Championships, he blasted through three opponents to reach the final, where he faced Hand again. Lesnar won this time, 2-1. "It was good to win this match," Lesnar said. "A 'W' is a 'W.'"

Still, the only real victory that mattered to Lesnar was available in two weeks. Lesnar traveled to St. Louis for the NCAA Championships, where he wanted to claim the ultimate prize. His parents were in attendance, along with his high school coach John Schiley. He defeated his first opponent by a 4-2 count, then pinned his next two foes. He won his semifinal match with another pin. Lesnar was in the championship match. His opponent was Hand once more. Lesnar led 1-0 after two periods. In the final round, Lesnar escaped to take a 2-0 lead. But late in the period, the referee penalized Lesnar a point for stalling. Then he penalized Lesnar another point for stalling again. The match was tied, 2-2. It went to overtime. Neither wrestler scored. It went to double overtime. With nine seconds remaining in the second overtime, Lesnar turned Hand around with a hip-heist to escape and win a point. He won, 3-2.

"When my hand was raised, winning the NCAA title, it was like a big weight was lifted off of me, and I had accomplished everything," said Lesnar. "I looked up at my mom and dad in the stands and I looked at my high school wrestling coach, and I (thought), 'Man, I did it. I finally did it.'"

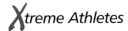

The next morning, Lesnar woke up in a panic. "I never felt so empty inside," he said. Lesnar had reached his ultimate goal. Now he had nothing to strive for. What in the world could he possibly do?

Lesnar had several options. He could try out for the Olympics. The 2000 Summer Olympic Games in Sydney, Australia, were approaching. But Lesnar knew that training with the U.S. Olympic Team and competing as an amateur for another half year meant not earning any money—and he was tired of being broke. He could switch to football. He still had a year of college eligibility, and Gophers coach Glen Mason had asked him to join the football team. But again, that meant no money. He could try pro football. He had talked with Tampa Bay Buccaneers coach Tony Dungy a few times, because Dungy had attended the University of Minnesota.

Fireworks over the Sydney Harbour Bridge during the closing ceremonies of the Olympic Games in Sydney, Australia, in 2000

Dungy had invited Lesnar to try out for the Buccaneers. But Lesnar wasn't sure he was ready to jump to pro football.

Lesnar decided he had one choice: pro wrestling. Gerry Brisco worked for the World Wrestling Federation (WWF), which is now known as World Wrestling Entertainment (WWE). Brisco met with Lesnar and coach Robinson about him joining the WWF.

Lesnar wanted to make sure he would be paid well and hired local attorney David Bradley Olsen to represent him. Olsen had worked for other professional wrestlers. Together they flew to Stamford, Connecticut, and the steely towers that housed the WWF. There they met with owner Vince McMahon and his lieutenants.

Lesnar says before his visit he hadn't watched five minutes of pro wrestling in his life, and the idea of acting out scripted matches seemed ridiculous. But he was impressed with the WWF headquarters and could tell immediately that McMahon was a smart businessman.

Still, Lesnar wasn't about to settle for just any sort of deal. He knew his six-foot-three-inch, 285-pound chiseled body and NCAA heavyweight title trophy made him a valuable piece of property for McMahon's wrestling organization. The two sides negotiated, and a final offer was made. Lesnar had to catch his breath. He signed his name immediately.

Vince McMahon

It is reported that he signed a multiyear deal worth several hundred thousand dollars per year. As Lesnar writes in his autobiography *Death Clutch: My Story of Determination, Domination, and Survival*, "I was being offered more money than I'd ever seen in my entire life. Brock Lesnar was off to join the circus!"

Fans show up by the thousands to see WWF action.

three
Get In to Get Out

Lesnar returned to Minneapolis to pay off his student loans and buy himself a motorcycle—a Harley-Davidson chopper. He contacted Brad Rheingans, a former pro wrestler and agent, to ask for guidance. Rheingans spent a few weeks teaching Lesnar some pro wrestling basics. Lesnar also met Curt Hennig, a popular pro who was known as Mr. Perfect. Hennig gave Lesnar some advice that Lesnar would never forget. Hennig's words were simple: "Get in to get out." Hennig explained that all the travel and other requirements of being a pro wrestler grinds you down, and the best way to keep your health is not to stay in the business longer than you think you should. It made sense to Lesnar.

One month later, on August 1, 2000, the WWF ordered Lesnar to report to Ohio Valley Wrestling (OVW), the company's developmental territory in Louisville, Kentucky, where he began training on how to perform moves like drop kicks and power slams.

Pro wrestling is scripted. The matches are planned out and rehearsed beforehand. The wrestlers know whether they are supposed to win or lose. Lesnar realized he wasn't so much an athlete now as he was an entertainer. He had always tried to dominate opponents for real. Now he had to follow a script. He had to almost brainwash himself in order to pull it off.

"It was strange at first," Lesnar said. "I had to go in with an open mind, keep [my mouth] shut and my ears open. I committed to myself. I committed to Vince McMahon. From the day I signed on the dotted line, I turned that switch, and I just wanted to become an entertainer."

After learning how to fall and make his punches and body slams appear real, Lesnar was put in the ring to start performing. He was teamed with former University of Minnesota wrestler Shelton Benjamin to form a tag team. Together Lesnar and Benjamin were made into an immediate success. They "defeated" the Disciples of Synn, B. J. Payne and Damien, to claim the OVW Southern Tag Team title. They lost the title two months later. Then they won it back.

Lesnar was performing well enough in the ring that on October 5, 2001, he got called up to be part of a crew at a WWF show in Winnipeg, Manitoba. Among the big names on the card were Kurt Angle, Chris Jericho, and Stone Cold Steve Austin.

Stone Cold Steve Austin

In mid-March 2002, Lesnar made his WWF television debut. He was teamed with Paul Heyman as his manager and spokesman. Heyman gave Lesnar the nickname "The Next Big Thing." Over the next two weeks, Lesnar performed run-ins, which were brief appearances in which he would jump in the ring, grab a wrestler, lift him up over his head, spin in a circle, and then come crashing down with him. The WWF called Lesnar's move the "F-5." Fans loved it. The WWF was creating its newest star. Lesnar was chosen by popular wrestler Ric Flair to join his RAW brand of the WWF.

Lesnar's life became a whirlwind. He traveled to towns in Pennsylvania, New Jersey, Texas, and elsewhere to perform almost nightly. He "won" most of his matches, defeating opponents like Spike, Bradshaw, Mr. Perfect, and the Hardy Boyz.

Most of Lesnar's time was spent traveling, getting more fans, and making more money. "Life on the road was wild," he said. "I was flying to a new city every day and living life like a rock star. Everywhere I went people knew me. I was having a great time, and who wouldn't? Money. Girls. More girls. More money."

After Lesnar beat the Hardy Boyz in May, in London, England, the WWF changed its name to World Wrestling Entertainment (WWE). But the acts stayed the same. A real incident happened on the plane flight back to the United States, however.

Lesnar was being scripted to become the next WWE heavyweight champion, and other wrestlers who had worked for years in the business without getting to be champion were jealous. Curt Hennig was especially furious. He taunted Lesnar, saying he could out-wrestle him for real. Lesnar and Hennig had to be separated. Hennig was fired from the WWE the next day. He died less than a year later at the age of forty-four.

In Atlanta one night, Lesnar could hardly believe the script. Owner Vince McMahon would fight legendary Ric Flair, with 50 percent ownership of the company at stake. It was all show, of course. The plan was that just as it appeared that Flair would win, Lesnar would jump in the ring and take down Flair to save his boss. McMahon would then be indebted to Lesnar and offer him a chance to win the WWE heavyweight title at SummerSlam. That's how it went down. Lesnar was on his way to becoming the champ.

On a TV episode of *Smackdown!*, Lesnar told Kurt Angle that his days of being champion were numbered. Lesnar was coming after him. On another *Smackdown!* episode, Lesnar beat superhero Hulk Hogan.

On August 25, 2002, at SummerSlam, Lesnar took on Dwayne "The Rock" Johnson. Lesnar's parents sat among the crowd at the Nassau Coliseum in Long Island, New York. They watched their son enter the ring in his black trunks and boots and perform twenty

minutes of falls and slams with The Rock. When Lesnar grabbed his opponent in a bearhug called the Brock Lock, the crowd roared.

At the age of twenty-five, Brock "The Next Big Thing" Lesnar was the youngest WWE heavyweight champion in history. Lesnar was thrilled. He knew he was an instant millionaire. "It wasn't about who was better, who would really win. Come on, that's ridiculous," Lesnar said. "It was about the fact I wanted to buy my mom and dad a house."

Lesnar had become a valuable property. He signed a seven-year contract with the WWE for $45 million. He began to spend his money, buying homes, cars, trucks, even an airplane. "It wasn't the same down-to-earth Brock I knew," said Marty Morgan, his former assistant coach at Minnesota. "He went from being an athlete to being in show business."

Lesnar competed in the biggest pay-per-view main events now. He defended his title against such heroes as The Undertaker, Triple H, the Big Show, and John Cena, and earned their respect for his ability to perform in the ring. "He's one of the best pure athletes I've ever seen," said Cena. "I think Brock Lesnar is the future of this company, his potential is unlimited."

Lesnar had appeared in WWE video games, but now he was being featured on the covers. He was fast becoming the most popular pro wrestler in the business. But life on the road was taking its toll on Lesnar.

Dwayne "The Rock" Johnson, right, delivers a "Rock Bottom" to WWE superstar John Cena in front of a sold-out crowd of 71,617 at the Georgia Dome.

He tried to stay fit by exercising in his hotel room, doing hundreds of push-ups and sit-ups a day. Soon it began to take a toll on his body, and he succumbed to relieving his pain with alcohol and painkillers. The question became: how long could he keep this up?

At Wrestlemania IXX, in Safeco Field in Seattle, Washington, Lesnar defeated Kurt Angle but not without nearly breaking his neck first. He climbed to the top rope of the ring and stood up to perform a Shooting Star Press. The crowd went wild as Lesnar launched himself feet first into a reverse somersault, but he overestimated the distance and slammed his head into Angle's side. Lesnar suffered a severe concussion. With Lesnar nearly unconscious, Angle changed the script and made himself lose immediately.

By now, Lesnar was starting a relationship with Rena Mero. She was better known as "Sable"—a popular wrestler in the Women's WWE. Brock and Rena married on May 6, 2006. They have two sons together—Turk (born in 2009) and Duke (2010). Lesnar and his former fiancé also have a daughter, Mya Lynn, born on April 10, 2002.

In the meantime, Lesnar was sensing that his time with the WWE was running out. He had spent a week at Dwayne "The Rock" Johnson's house in Miami going over the script for an upcoming bout. However, the finish hadn't been written in the script, and he wondered why.

In the dressing room at the arena an hour before the main event, Lesnar and The Rock were rehearsing their battle. Lesnar still didn't know how he was supposed to win the fight and was stunned when The Rock said, "and that's when I'll hit you with the Rock Bottom, one . . . two . . . three." Lesnar laughed. He thought The Rock was joking. If he got counted out, that meant he would lose. He was the champ. He couldn't lose. Could he? He saw that The Rock was not kidding. Then it hit him. He was being shifted sideways. Vince McMahon was bringing in another fresh face.

Lesnar was outraged. Why hadn't McMahon told him himself? In the ring, Lesnar acted out his loss as he was told, but he never trusted McMahon again. He told McMahon he wanted out of the WWE and agreed to one last fight. At Wrestlemania XX, at Madison Square Garden in New York, Lesnar lost to Bill Goldberg, as planned. Lesnar was relieved to be free from the WWE.

"It was gratifying at first, living life as a rock star, but it just wasn't the life for me," he said. "I couldn't stand myself the way I was living. I'm an outdoors kind of guy. I like to hunt. I like to fish. I found myself in an airport four days a week and in a different hotel room and arena every night. It wasn't for me."

In a surprising turn, Lesnar immediately set his sights on pro football. Red McCombs, the owner of

Lesnar (69) leaves the field after exchanging handshakes with San Francisco 49ers players.

the Minnesota Vikings, also happened to be a fan of pro wrestling and knew about Lesnar. McCombs urged the Vikings coaches to give Lesnar a tryout.

Lesnar joined the Vikings at their 2004 training camp. "This is no load of bull; it's no WWE stunt," Lesnar told a Minneapolis radio station. "I am dead serious about this. I ain't afraid of anything, and I ain't afraid of anybody. I'm as good an athlete as a lot of guys in the NFL, if not better."

Lesnar drew gasps from the Vikings in the weight room by benching 475 pounds and squatting seven hundred. His performance on the field was another story. He played on the defensive line and was con-fused with basic maneuvers, even how to line up. "We've started with Lesnar at Point A," defensive line coach Jim Panagos told reporters. "You guys wanna know what Point A is? Point A is the stance."

In a scrimmage against the Kansas City Chiefs, Lesnar hit quarterback Damon Huard late, draw-ing the ire of the Chiefs. In a preseason game at the Metrodome against the San Francisco 49ers, Lesnar got to play late in the fourth quarter and registered his first tackle on the final play of the game, which drew a standing ovation from the home crowd.

There was simply too much for Lesnar to learn, and the team cut him before the season started. He hugged head coach Mike Tice and thanked him for the opportunity. He left an impression on the Vikings.

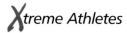

"When we signed him, I was skeptical," said lineman Chris Hovan. "I thought signing him was just a publicity stunt by either the club or the WWE. But Lesnar didn't come in here thinking he was a big shot. He took it seriously and kept his mouth shut. Nobody worked harder." On the evening Lesnar got cut, he was in the wilderness bow-hunting whitetail deer.

Lesnar couldn't sit still for long. He wanted to earn money. Pro wrestling was what he knew best, but he didn't want to go back to the WWE. He decided to join New Japan Pro Wrestling. But there was a big obstacle. When Lesnar left the WWE, he signed a no-compete clause. According to court documents, it meant that he was not allowed to compete "in the business of professional wrestling, ultimate fighting, and/or sports entertainment in any capacity whatsoever through June 30, 2010."

The WWE was basically claiming to "own" him. Lesnar may have been foolish to sign such an agreement and now regretted doing so. He needed to be allowed to participate in other sports or promotions.

In February 2005, Lesnar sued the WWE to reclaim his right to work. His attorney, David Olson, said, "Brock needs to get back to work. Wrestling and contact sports are what he knows." The WWE counter-sued, claiming that if Lesnar worked for any other "non-WWE sports entertainment company in the world before 2010," it would cause the company "irreparable harm." The court process dragged out through the summer with both sides finally appearing to reach an agreement.

Lesnar thought he was free to wrestle, and on October 8, 2005, he competed in a pay-per-view event at the Tokyo Dome for New Japan Pro Wrestling. He defeated Kazuyuki Fujita and Masa Chono to win the International Wrestling Grand Prix (IWGP) heavyweight title. The IWGP is the promotion's top title, and for New Japan Pro Wrestling to give Lesnar that

The Tokyo Dome

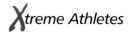

title at the very start showed his value to the outfit. The WWE was furious. They filed a restraining order to try to stop Lesnar from wrestling for another promotion.

While attorneys for both sides argued, rumors swirled that Total Nonstop Action Wrestling (TNA) wanted Lesnar to join its promotion. TNA was the WWE's stiffest rival. Losing Lesnar to the TNA would be a disaster for the WWE.

Meanwhile, Lesnar defended his IWGP heavyweight title in December on back-to-back nights with wins over Manabu Nakanishi and Yuji Nagata. Less than three weeks later, the WWE withdrew its request for the restraining order, allowing Lesnar to continue performing for New Japan. On January 4, 2006, with an estimated 40,000 fans in attendance at the Tokyo Dome, Lesnar defended his IWGP heavyweight title by defeating Shinsuke Nakamura.

Ten days later, a judge warned the WWE that unless it presented a better argument for trying to prevent Lesnar from competing for other organizations, it would rule in favor of Lesnar. Attorneys for Lesnar and the WWE reached a settlement soon after. While terms were not disclosed, both sides said they were pleased with the agreement. On June 12, a federal judge dismissed Lesnar's lawsuit after both sides requested that the case be dismissed. It is believed that Lesnar and the WWE agreed that Lesnar could compete in any other sport, including mixed martial arts, but that if he participated in pro wrestling, it could only be with a promotion outside the United States. This essentially protected the WWE's interest in not allowing Lesnar to join rival TNA.

This agreement fit perfectly into Lesnar's plans. He had little interest in pro wrestling at this point. He was just using New Japan to make easy money. His eye was on the future. He wanted to compete in a real sport, and that sport was mixed martial arts.

Lesnar strikes a pose at a weigh-in.

Proving Ground

I n July 2006, Lesnar started an intense training program in mixed martial arts (MMA). He hired two experts—Marty Morgan and Greg Nelson. Morgan, an assistant wrestling coach at the University of Minnesota, coordinated Lesnar's training program. Nelson, who ran an MMA academy in Minneapolis, taught Lesnar striking skills from such disciplines as Muay Thai, kickboxing, and especially Brazilian Jiu-Jitsu. Lesnar trained twice daily—practicing fighting skills in the morning and doing strength training and running in the evening. Lesnar's fierce desire and potential for success impressed both instructors. "He's stubborn, but he listens," said Morgan. Nelson agreed, and said, "He has tons of upper-body strength, but also has strong hips, which helps with takedowns and positioning, and footwork that [enable] him to sprawl and scramble."

In August, Lesnar signed a deal with an MMA promotion called K-1. Three months later, K-1 announced that Lesnar would make his mixed martial arts debut at the Los Angeles Memorial Coliseum. The fight was set for June 2. Lesnar's opponent would be a mammoth-sized fighter named Hong-Man Choi, who was seven feet two inches and weighed 319 pounds.

One week before the contest, Choi failed his pre-fight physical. The California State Athletic Commission would not allow him to compete. Lesnar's new opponent would be Min-Soo Kim, an Olympic silver-medal winner in judo.

With an estimated 52,000 fans in attendance and millions more watching on the television cable network Showtime, Lesnar entered the Octagon for the first time. He was being paid $500,000 for the fight.

At the opening bell, Lesnar went straight at Kim and took him to the ground. He mounted Kim and passed his guard, then began pounding him with punches to the head. With relentless fury, he landed lefts and rights directly into Kim's temples. Just one minute and nine seconds into the fight, Kim tapped out.

Afterward, Lesnar was interviewed in the ring. As he talked, a wad of chewing tobacco bulged from behind his lower lip. Lesnar told the crowd that he wished he could face Choi in the future, but that he was ready to join the promotion that wanted him most. Lesnar had already been in talks with Ultimate

Lesnar (right) battles Min-Soo Kim from South Korea during fight action at the Los Angeles Coliseum.

Fighting Championship (UFC) president Dana White. The UFC was the most popular mixed martial arts promotion in the world. Lesnar considered this contest for K-1 a chance for him to showcase his ability. Now that he had raised his value he knew he would soon be hearing from White.

In the meantime, Lesnar was invited back to New Japan Pro Wrestling for what would be his final match. Lesnar agreed to defend, and relinquish, his IWGP heavyweight title. On June 29, 2007, at the Tokyo Sumo Hall, Lesnar allowed Kurt Angle to pin him with an ankle lock, thereby surrendering his title. It was Lesnar's last pro wrestling performance.

On October 20, during UFC 77 in Cincinnati, Ohio, the announcement came: Brock Lesnar had joined the UFC. He signed a two-year contract with the promotion. His first fight would be in February 2008.

Lesnar appeared on the cover of *Muscle & Fitness*, and in the article inside the magazine, he explained what took him so long to start fighting for real:

> I would have done it to begin with, but there was really nothing going on with MMA when I was coming out of college. If I would've gone into it then, by now I could have forty fights under my belt

and most of my teeth missing and nothing to show for it. I'm in it at the right
time. This is getting to be nearly the biggest sport in the world. The bottom line is
Vince offered me a contract (in the WWE)
with guaranteed money, and I was tired of
being broke. I did it at the right time, and
I got out at the right time. Now I'm doing
this at the right time, too.

Some fans were skeptical. They saw Lesnar as a
sort of cartoon character created by the phony world
of the WWE. Winning one K-1 promotion fight did
not mean he could survive in the ultra-competitive
UFC against the best fighters in the world. Lesnar
saw it differently:

I'm in this for the long haul. I think MMA
was what I was always meant to do, and
I'm willing to work harder than anyone
else to be the best. I've always been the
hardest worker. That's how I've gotten
where I am in life. Now, in the UFC, I've
got the ideal job. I get paid to beat people
up. What could be better than that?

Can a boxer beat a judo expert? Can a wrestler beat a karate black belt? Sports fans often wondered such things. On November 12, 1993, at McNichols Sports Arena in Denver, Colorado, a contest was held to find out. The idea was hatched by ad man Art Davie and martial arts master Rorion Gracie. They called it War of the Worlds. Semaphore Entertainment Group (SEG) televised the event on pay-per-view. A SEG employee referred to it as the Ultimate Fighting Championship, and the name stuck. The event was later renamed UFC 1: The Beginning. The eight-man, single-elimination tournament featured, among other disciplines, two kickboxers, a shootfighter, and a sumo wrestler. The winner was Royce Gracie, a Brazilian Jiu Jitsu black belt and Rorion's younger brother. The event drew 86,592 TV subscribers which was considered a success.

"That show was only supposed to be a one-off," current UFC president Dana White said. "It did so well on pay-per-view they decided to do another, and another. Never in a million years did these guys think they were creating a sport." Four months later, a sixteen-man tournament called UFC 2: No Way Out was held with Gracie winning again.

The early UFC bouts had no weight classes, matching fighters of widely varying sizes. Two separate weight classes (heavyweight two hundred pounds; lightweight 199 and under) were introduced in 1997. There were only three ways to end a fight—knockout, submission, or throwing in the towel. That is, there were no decisions, and consequently, no judges.

One fight at UFC 5: The Return of the Beast was a singles fight and so was not part of the tournament. That fight, between Royce Gracie and Ken Shamrock, lasted more than thirty-six minutes and had to be declared a draw because both fighters became too exhausted to continue. The tournament style was phased out in 1998, with all contests held as singles fights.

The UFC touted its combat sport with the phrase "There are no rules!" and disallowed only biting and eye gouging. The early fights permitted groin strikes, head-butting, and fish-hooking (finger-ripping the cheeks), among other violent techniques.

Government authorities stepped in to legislate the sport, and many states outlawed it. Stricter rules were implemented to ease concerns. The sport experienced moderate success, but SEG was on the verge of bankruptcy, and so advertising was minimal. In 2001, Station Casinos executives Frank and Lorenzo Fertitta bought the UFC for $2 million and created Zuffa, LLC as its parent company (zuffa means "to fight" in Italian). Dana White was named president and given 9 percent ownership.

Lorenzo Fertitta was a former member of the Nevada State Athletic Commission, and his connections influenced that state to allow events to be held at ritzy casinos. Zuffa invested heavily in promotions. Visibility was increased in 2005 with the creation of a reality television show, *The Ultimate Fighter (TUF)*, which aired on Spike TV to much fanfare. A second weekly program, *UFC Unleashed*, followed. UFC's pay-per-view buy rate exploded. In 2006, the promotion generated more than $222,766,000 in pay-per-view revenue, surpassing both boxing and pro wrestling. That same year, Zuffa bought out competitor World Fighting Alliance. Japan-based rival Pride Fighting Championships was acquired one year later. In 2010, the UFC merged with its sister promotion, World Extreme Cagefighting. In 2011, Zuffa purchased rival Strikeforce. Zuffa controlled all relevant promotions now and nearly all the world's top-ranked fighters. The UFC was king of mixed martial arts.

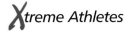

It was revealed in January that Lesnar's opponent for his debut fight with the UFC would be Frank Mir. Mir became a UFC legend when he snapped a man's arm in a 2004 fight. That same year he won the UFC heavyweight title. A motorcycle accident temporarily halted his reign, but now he was fully recovered and winning again.

The event was called UFC 81: Breaking Point. It was held February 2, 2008, at the Mandalay Bay Events Center in Las Vegas, Nevada. There were nine fights on the card, including a heavyweight title fight between Antonio Rodrigo Nogueira and Tim Sylvia.

Lesnar's match with Mir was billed as the main event. What's more, even though this was Lesnar's first fight for the UFC, he was being paid $250,000, more than any other fighter on the card. Several days before the fight, Lesnar said:

> There are some people who disapprove of where I'm at on the card because of who I am. There is going to be a lot of animosity toward me because of the visibility that I have. I've got to come out and prove myself, even to the other fighters. I've got a lot to prove. All I have to do right now is shut up and play ball and keep on proving myself.

A crowd of 10,583 filled the Mandalay Bay arena. The front rows featured UFC superstars George St. Pierre, Chuck "The Iceman" Liddell, Quinton "Rampage" Jackson, BJ Penn, and Matt Hughes. WWE heroes Stone Cold Steve Austin, Kurt Angle, and The Undertaker were there to support Lesnar. The fight received an estimated 600,000 pay-per-view buys, which was the most for an event in 2008.

The crowd roared from the start when Lesnar shot out like a missile to take down Mir. Lesnar smashed Mir's head with several vicious punches, and it

Brock Lesnar, right, battles Frank Mir in the first round of their UFC heavyweight bout Saturday, February 2, 2008, in Las Vegas.

appeared that Mir might tap out at any moment. But then Lesnar accidentally hit Mir in the back of the head, which is not allowed. Referee Steve Mazzagatti stopped the fight, stood the fighters up, and deducted a point from Lesnar for an illegal strike.

The bout resumed with Lesnar in control again, but he left his right leg free, and Mir locked in a kneebar. Suddenly Lesnar was helpless. Mir squeezed Lesnar's leg back. Lesnar's leg was about to be snapped like a carrot. In a panic, Lesnar tapped out. The match lasted ninety seconds.

Lesnar was stunned. He knew he was the more powerful man. Mir showed him that mixed martial arts fighting is more than just brute strength. As one publication clearly described it, "Lesnar was bigger, possibly more skilled, and much meaner than Mir. In the end it wasn't Mir; it was Brock's own enthusiasm that got the best of him."

After the match, Dana White said, "The question surrounding this event was can Brock Lesnar fight and I think the answer is yes, he can." One publication described the fight this way: "Man versus beast, and the man was getting hammered into oblivion and managed to capitalize on a single mistake the monster made to get the victory."

Lesnar said later that he didn't think the referee needed to stop the fight for the single accidental punch. White agreed, saying, "That referee has no business being in this business."

Although Lesnar lost the fight, he won over critics who thought he couldn't compete against a formidable foe. It was a moral victory of sorts, and Lesnar could either pout or learn from it. He went right back to training, more committed than ever to winning.

A few months after the loss, Lesnar said:

> I'm still disgusted with myself. I got so excited, then for Mazzagatti to stop the fight kinda threw a monkey wrench into my rhythm a little bit, and thus you chalk it up to a little bit of inexperience. I had Frank in a dominant position, and I stood up and fed him a foolish, amateur mistake. I think Frank will be the first one to admit that I had him up against the ropes, and I think he was scared.

Brock Lesnar, top, pounds away at Randy Couture.

five

"Can You See Me Now?"

Lesnar stewed over his loss to Mir as he trained through the spring and into the summer. He had recently moved with Rena from his home in the Minneapolis area 110 miles away to the small town of Alexandria. He preferred living in a relatively remote area. He has always wanted to maintain his privacy. He is not on Facebook, does not have a Twitter account, and rarely watches TV. He doesn't own a computer and never uses the Internet. "The people that I care about," he says. "They know where to find me if they need me."

Lesnar's house in Alec, as the locals call it, sits on a forty-acre ranch with a large converted warehouse that serves as his training center. The gym features strength training equipment, treadmills, and wrestling mats.

Lesnar named his organization Death Clutch, and he paid a crew of trainers and sparring partners to live in his guesthouse and help train him. Greg Nelson oversaw his program, while Marty Morgan served as his main wrestling and head coach. Erik Paulson was his submission wrestling and kickboxing coach. Rodrigo Mederios was his Brazilian Jiu-Jitsu coach ,and Peter Welch was his boxing coach. Together, Lesnar's team prepared him for his next fight.

Lesnar's chance to get his career on track arrived on August 9, 2008, at UFC 87: Seek and Destroy, which was held at the Target Center in Minneapolis, Minnesota. Ticket prices ranged from fifty dollars to six hundred dollars, and the crowd of 15,042 produced $2.25 million in gate receipts for the UFC. The company made millions more with pay-per-view buys.

Lesnar's fight with veteran "Texas Crazy Horse" Heath Herring was a co-main event, much to the delight of the fans who considered him a hometown favorite from his days as a wrestler at the University of Minnesota. Herring had forty-three mixed martial arts fights to his credit, and he was capable of capitalizing on any mistake Lesnar made. On the other hand, Herring was no threat to overwhelm Lesnar. While the UFC's bouts were absolutely real, the matchups were designed somewhat to extend a more attractive fighter's career. After all, the promotion's focus was to sell tickets and attract pay-per-view purchases.

The UFC certainly recognized Lesnar's marketability. They knew if Lesnar lost two fights in a row, given his background in the fake WWE, fans would not take him seriously. So they matched him up with a wise, but average, opponent.

Lesnar was eager to put on a show, but he was careful not to leave himself open for a fluke submission. To start the fight, he shot at Herring with a wild knee, but he quickly righted himself and moments later came in with a thunderous straight right hand that floored Herring. Lesnar smothered Herring, who tried to escape by sliding up the cage. Lesnar pulled him back down and controlled him on the ground with his strength and wrestling technique and spent nearly the entire five minutes of the round delivering head punches and body knees. So many ferocious blows nearly sent Herring into unconsciousness. Lesnar's fists are so huge that he wears 4XL gloves, the largest of any MMA fighter in history, and Herring learned firsthand the force of Lesnar's hammerfists.

In the second round, Herring was back on the ground. Midway through, his face was a bloody pulp. He managed to get to his feet, but Lesnar put him up against the cage and delivered two jarring knees to his midsection. Herring grimaced and crumpled back to the ground.

In the third and final round, Herring stood up with Lesnar for a moment, but Lesnar's sheer size was too much. Herring collapsed under Lesnar's weight. Lesnar smartly played it safe now by locking up Herring from a side position and blasting him with an occasional punch to the face. The final bell came, and with it, certain victory. Lesnar pointed a finger at Herring and then embraced the fighter. All three judges scored the fight 30-26 to give Lesnar a unanimous decision.

Interviewed in the Octagon afterward, Lesnar said, "I fell off the horse against Frank Mir and tonight I got on that stallion and rode out of town. I've just been trying to work on everything, every single day to get better, to be a well-rounded heavyweight fighter and a contender in the UFC." Then Lesnar turned to the crowd and yelled "Can you see me now? Can you see me now?" His hometown fans roared with delight.

Lesnar did not celebrate for long. He wanted something more—the heavyweight championship belt—and his opportunity came sooner than some thought it should. When it was announced that Lesnar would next face Randy Couture for the UFC heavyweight title, several veteran fighters groused about it. Lesnar responded:

> I'm getting sick of hearing from some
> dumb people [who] say I don't deserve
> this fight because I've only been fighting
> for a year. My message to them is simple:
> Get over it! This is a business, and people
> know who I am and want to see me fight.

UFC 91: Couture vs. Lesnar was held November
15, 2008, at the MGM Grand Garden Arena in Las
Vegas. Celebrities such as rapper 50 Cent, baseball
slugger Ryan Howard, and actress Mandy Moore
ringed the Octagon. Couture was forty-five years old
and hadn't fought in nearly fifteen months due to a
contract dispute with the UFC. But he was a savvy
veteran who had either defended or fought for a championship in thirteen of his past fourteen bouts, and he
was the defending heavyweight champion.

Lesnar knew from the start he was in for a royal
battle. "Honest to God, up till when they said 'Let's
go,' I was pretty nervous," Lesnar said. "We watched
a lot of film on Randy, and we broke it down. I didn't
really know what to expect."

Lesnar took down the champion with a double leg
to start the fight, but when he tried to mount, Couture
reversed him. Lesnar was able to reverse back, but
he couldn't keep Couture underneath him. Worse for
Lesnar, each time the fighters broke their clinches,

Randy Couture takes a few final punches from Lesnar, top, during the second round of their UFC World Heavyweight match on November 15, 2008, in Las Vegas.

Couture managed to deliver the quicker punches. Late in the first round, one of Couture's strikes cut Lesnar above his eye. Lesnar noticed he was leaking blood. He said:

> Right away, it made me a little nervous, but then it pissed me off. I wanted to get first blood on Randy. Any time you fight, you want to get first blood. Something in my head just went, 'Alright, we've got to pick this up.' And that's what I did.

In the second round, Lesnar delivered two vicious blows. One was a short but massive elbow that staggered Couture. The other was a straight right that collapsed Couture to the ground. "Honestly, I didn't see it," Couture said of the punch that sent him to the canvas. "Next thing I know I was on the ground eating leather. My corner told me it looked like it caught me behind the ear." Lesnar fell onto Couture and began wailing away. He landed nearly forty hammerfists before referee Mario Yamasaki mercifully stopped the fight on a technical knockout at 3:07 of the second round.

Lesnar jumped to his feet and threw his arms in the air. He climbed up the cage and saluted the crowd. "I can't believe it," he said afterward. "I can't believe it." Couture certainly could believe it after spending eight minutes in the Octagon with Lesnar. "Guys aren't just big anymore, they're very good athletes," he said. "Brock is a great indication of where the division is going."

Just four fights into his mixed martial arts career, Lesnar was the UFC heavyweight champion. Lesnar's popularity was soaring, and he could have stayed in the glitz of Las Vegas to soak it up. But the morning after his triumph, he was headed back home to the quiet of his ranch in Alexandria. A few days after that, he was hunting in the wilderness. Lesnar was not in the UFC for the attention; he was in it to be champion.

At UFC 92, Frank Mir defeated Antonio Rodrigo Nogueira. Lesnar was seated ringside. Mir walked toward Lesnar and shouted, "You've got my belt." The stage was set for a classic showdown. Lesnar could hardly wait. He wanted revenge.

The rematch between Lesnar and Mir was originally planned for May 2009, but Mir suffered a knee injury during training, and the fight was postponed. It was rescheduled for July 11, the day before Lesnar's birthday. It would be the main event at UFC 100: Lesnar vs. Mir 2 at the Mandalay Bay Events Center. Lesnar would receive $400,000 for the fight. Mir would get $45,000.

Before the fight, Mir said:

> Brock Lesnar has been calling for a rematch with me ever since I beat him the first time. All I can say to Brock is be careful what you wish for because I'm a better, smarter, stronger, and faster fighter than I was the last time.

Mir was filled with confidence, which is a necessary quality for a fighter to be successful, but he seemed to be taking Lesnar too lightly. According to FightMetric statistics, Lesnar had out-struck his opponents nearly five-to-one, and he connected on sixty-two of seventy-two power strikes, making Lesnar the most accurate ground striker in UFC history. Mir was not impressed:

> He's fought for an additional, what, 22 minutes, since the time we faced each other. That's not a whole lot of time. I mean, he's fought two fights since then. We all know that it takes a long time to really become cage-savvy.

Lesnar's trainer, Greg Nelson, knew otherwise. Much had changed for Lesnar in the seventeen months since he faced Mir the first time. Nelson said:

Obviously, Brock then was a really raw athlete. He had a great wrestling background and just a competitive ferocity about him. You could see that in the ring. He just exploded, went out there, and just as fast as you light that fuse, the fire blew up and then it was over. Now you've got a great athlete who's really explosive, but now he's added really good striking, and a very technical and strong grappling game, on top of his wrestling.

The Mandalay Bay was packed for the rematch, and it generated 1.6 million pay-per-view buys, the most ever for a UFC event. Lesnar had lost to Mir with a kneebar, and sure enough, in the first minute this time, Mir grabbed for Lesnar's knee again. Lesnar was ready for it. He thwarted Mir's grab and took Mir to the ground. He held Mir in a half guard for the rest of the first round and landed some especially painful head and body shots in the closing seconds to bloody Mir's face.

The second round was far more violent. Mir connected with a short left hand and then a knee and a jumping knee. Then Lesnar took over. He took Mir to the ground again and rolled Mir onto his side against the cage and trapped an arm. Then he pounded him

Lesnar, right, and Frank Mir battle for the UFC 100 Heavyweight Title.

with a barrage of right hands until referee Herb Dean called a halt to the bout at 1:48 of the second round.

Lesnar had taken his revenge. Unfortunately, he did not let his action speak for itself. He reverted back to the pro wrestling days and purposely played the role of the villain. First, he taunted Mir, and the two fighters had to be separated. Next, he paraded around the Octagon and gestured with his fingers to a booing crowd that just grew louder with its displeasure toward him. UFC interviewer Joe Rogan put the microphone into his face, and Lesnar said, "I love it. Keep going. I love it, man." Then he criticized the UFC's main sponsor and made more lewd comments. The crowd booed lustily.

Lesnar left the Octagon to a cascade of boos. He wondered what he had just done. In the bathroom of his dressing room afterward, UFC president Dana White angrily confronted Lesnar. White told Lesnar that his behavior was outrageous and made it clear that such a stunt would not be tolerated again.

At the post-fight press conference, White said, "Brock went so far over the top tonight I can't even describe it. I don't think in the history of the UFC we've ever done anything like that. You don't act like something you're not. This isn't the WWE. I don't ask these guys to act crazy so we can get more pay-per-views. That's not the business I'm in."

Lesnar knew he had blown it. He apologized at the press conference and said his antics were partly due to him being so hyped to exact revenge on Mir. "I'm a sore loser," Lesnar explained. "I don't like to get beat. I acted very unprofessionally after the fight. I screwed up."

Lesnar, right, and Frank Mir

SIX

Near-Death and Back

The criticism for Lesnar's behavior was swift and heavy. Veteran Randy Couture expressed the thoughts of many UFC fighters when he said, "I don't know if he lost his mind or what happened. The athletes in our sport don't act that way. We've spent a long time building a reputation of sportsmanship. It was disappointing to see. I was disgusted."

WWE vice president and announcer Jim Ross said:

> Those that do not personally know Lesnar as I do need to understand that his level of intensity and fury is scary. Lesnar has said many things in private conversations that I have been a part of that would make one do a double take. He is an intimidating, emotional jock who has been known for speaking first and thinking later.

UFC Basics

UFC matches are held in an eight-sided cage called an Octagon. The Octagon is thirty-two feet wide. The fence is made of black vinyl similar in form to a playground fence and is five-and-one-half feet high. Two gates are on opposite sides of the fence. During the match, only the two fighters and the referee are allowed inside the Octagon. Between rounds, assistants (cornermen) are permitted inside to provide treatment and advice.

Rounds are five minutes each. A contest for a championship belt is five rounds. All other matches are three rounds. There is a one-minute rest between rounds. Fighters are grouped into classes based on weight. The seven weight divisions are bantamweight (126 to 135 pounds), featherweight (136-145), lightweight (146-155), welterweight (156-170), middleweight (171-185), light heavyweight (186-205), and heavyweight (206-265). Fighters must wear approved shorts and open-fingered gloves with padding at least one-inch thick around the knuckles. Nothing else can be worn.

A view of the UFC Octagon

Fights are decided in four ways:

Submission

The fighter declares quitting by tapping on the mat or his opponent. This is commonly known as tapping out.

Knockout (KO)

The fighter loses consciousness.

Technical Knockout (TKO)

The fighter is declared finished by the referee when, in the referee's judgment the fighter no longer has the ability to defend himself, the ringside doctor calls it due to excessive bleeding or serious injury, or the fighter's own cornermen signals to end the bout.

Judge's Decision

On a fight that goes the distance, three judges score the fight and render their decision. If all three judges agree on the winner, it is a unanimous decision. If two judges agree on the winner, while the other judge declares it a tie, it is a majority decision. If two judges agree on the winner, while the other judge scores a win for the loser, it is a split decision. If the scoring comes out equal, it is a draw (tie).

State athletic commissions and the UFC work together to enforce a long list of fouls. Among the most flagrant are head-butting, eye-gouging, hair-pulling, biting, groin attacks, fish-hooking, throat strikes, clawing, pinching, and kicking or kneeing the head of a grounded opponent.

Lesnar's behavior cast him as a villain, and Dana White was sure to explain to his emerging superstar that, unlike pro wrestling, the UFC did not need such characters. White also knew that too much negative attention was not good for his sport and quickly tried to redirect the focus to Lesnar's fighting ability. "This guy is a phenomenal athlete," he told reporters, "and he gets better every time. He might be the greatest heavyweight champion in history." It was a bold statement, but who could argue?

White and his team scheduled Lesnar's next match for November 2009. His opponent would be unbeaten Shane Carwin, a skilled athlete who earned college All-American honors in football and wrestling. In his blog, Carwin called Lesnar's behavior after the Mir fight "lame." Carwin wrote:

> He may be champion, but he has a long ways to go before he earns the respect of a champion . . . We have no scripts in this sport. It doesn't matter if you win or lose; it matters how you win or lose.

The criticism bothered Lesnar. He was eager to put the incident behind him, but as he trained for the Carwin match, something didn't seem quite right. He routinely worked out hard enough that his energy was spent afterward, but normally he perked back up within an hour. Now he stayed tired afterward and even grew tired right in the middle of workouts. His stomach ached and before long, he was tired all the time. Some days he could barely get out of bed. He dragged himself to the doctor where he was diagnosed with mononucleosis. The doctor recommended a long rest. Lesnar had to postpone his fight with Carwin.

On October 26, Dana White announced that the Lesnar-Carwin fight was being postponed because Lesnar was too ill to train. "He said he's never been this sick in his life," White said. "He said it's been going on for a long time, and he just wasn't able to shake it." Fans everywhere wanted to know what was wrong with Lesnar. Speculation was rampant. It was rumored that he had mononucleosis or something worse. Carwin guessed that he had a bird flu called H1N1. White told reporters that Lesnar didn't have AIDS or cancer.

Lesnar was disappointed to let the UFC down. He decided to take his family to western Manitoba for a relaxing weekend of hunting. The first night he woke up in excruciating pain and was sweating profusely. He told Rena that he needed to get to a hospital right away. He couldn't stand up on his own.

Luckily, Lesnar's brother Chad was there, and he carried Lesnar to the car. At the hospital, Lesnar was

administered morphine to ease the pain. An X-ray of his stomach was taken, but it provided no answer to his ailment. A CT scan was needed, but the machine was broken. A part was needed to repair it. Lesnar was told the part would arrive in the morning.

Lesnar lay in the hospital bed with Rena at his side, suffering horribly. He was fed chicken broth, but vomited it back up. The day went by. The part didn't come. Lesnar was assured it was coming. The night was long, and he grew sicker.

The next morning, the part still had not arrived. Lesnar was afraid for his life. He and Rena decided to go to another hospital. Rena drove one hundred miles per hour for four hours to the nearest hospital in Bismarck, North Dakota. The drive was sheer agony for Lesnar.

Within the first half hour at Med Center One, Lesnar had been given a CT scan and was diagnosed with diverticulitis. He also had a severe bacterial infection caused by a hole in his stomach. His body was being poisoned by his own fecal matter.

Lesnar was given heavy medication, but if it didn't work within eight hours, he would need to undergo a major operation. Fortunately, the medication worked, but he still had a hole in his stomach and spent the next eleven days in the hospital with no food or liquid. An intravenous drip delivered nutrients to his body to keep him alive.

Lesnar with his wife Rena

In mid-November, White told fans that Lesnar may never compete in the UFC again. "He's in rough shape, he's in really bad shape," White said. "He is not well and he is not getting any better. He's very, very sick. He's got a lot of problems."

When Lesnar was released from the hospital, he was too weak to walk, so he was rolled out in a wheelchair. He looked at Rena and said, "The world's baddest man, huh?" At least he could laugh about it.

Dana White

Lesnar had a follow-up examination at the Mayo Clinic in Rochester, Minnesota, where surgery was suggested. Lesnar asked if he could wait to see if his body might heal somewhat on its own. Although he was told to take it easy he began to work out again. He worked out slowly at first, walking on a treadmill and lifting light dumbbells. He slowly increased his workout load. More important, he changed his diet by eliminating processed foods and adding more fruits and vegetables.

One month later, he returned to the Mayo Clinic for a checkup. Doctors were amazed at the results. Surgery was no longer necessary, and Lesnar's recovery appeared complete. Lesnar was thankful not just to get a green light to resume his UFC career but to also know he could be a healthy husband and father. He says his near-death experience made him appreciate his family more and gave him a new lease on life.

Lesnar resumed training for his fight with Carwin, which was scheduled as the main event at UFC 116: Lesnar vs. Carwin. Lesnar kept his regular team of coaches and hired two more: Luke Richesson for strength and conditioning and Peter Welch for boxing. He had lost forty pounds from his illness, but by the time the fight arrived, he had gained more than thirty back, most of it muscle.

The fight was held July 3, 2010, at the MGM Grand Garden Arena. Carwin was a six-foot-five-inch, 280-pound former All-American linebacker who was unbeaten at 12-0 in the UFC. All of his victories ended in the first round. Carwin said before the fight, "If I touch anybody with my hands, I can knock them out."

Lesnar didn't blink. The way he saw it, he had just beaten diverticulitis, a far tougher opponent than Carwin. He said:

> I could have just hung it up, stayed at home and been a family man. It's not how I want my career to end. If this thing's going to stop, I want it to be on my terms. I just don't see Shane Carwin as being a guy that's going to stop this freight train.

But Lesnar was nearly derailed by Carwin in the first round. At the opening bell, he charged in but was unable to take down Carwin, who responded by clocking Lesnar with a knee to the head. Carwin next rocked Lesnar on the chin with a straight right hand and a left uppercut that sent the champ staggering into the cage. Carwin then took Lesnar to the ground and pounded him with fists for two solid minutes, opening a nasty cut over Lesnar's left eye. With blood gushing down his face, Lesnar somehow managed to stand up and fend off Carwin to the bell.

Lesnar, left, takes a knee from Shane Carwin during
their UFC heavyweight mixed martial arts title match.

"I just had to go into survival mode," Lesnar said after the fight. The good thing was that Carwin was spent after exerting so much energy in the first round. At the start of the second round, Lesnar smiled and high-fived Carwin. Then he shot in at Carwin and took him down. Lesnar gained a full mount, then moved into side-control and put Carwin in an arm triangle choke that had all his weight pushing down on Carwin. At the 2:19 mark, Carwin tapped.

In the Octagon afterward, Lesnar was thankful, exactly the opposite of how he acted after his win over Mir. "This is about my family," he told the crowd. "This is about my doctors. This is about my training partners. I am blessed by God. I stand before you a humble champion, and I'm still the toughest (guy) around, baby." This time, the crowd cheered.

Three months later, the cheering for Lesnar stopped, at least for the moment. At UFC 121: Lesnar vs. Velasquez, at the Honda Center in Anaheim, California, Lesnar was beaten by the hard-hitting Cain Velasquez. Lesnar took down the smaller Velasquez twice in the first round, but he couldn't hold the elusive fighter down. Velasquez corralled Lesnar from behind and landed a brutal barrage of punches. Somehow Lesnar got back to his feet, but a one-two combination dropped him again. Velasquez pounded away until referee Herb Dean stepped in to stop the assault at 4:12 of the opening round.

Lesnar was gracious, saying, "I knew there was a great challenge in front of me. He's a great fighter. What can I say? He was better than me tonight."

Lesnar resumed training with the sole intent of somehow reclaiming his title belt. One month later, White invited Lesnar to be a coach on the thirteenth season of the TV program *The Ultimate Fighter* against Junior dos Santos. After the episodes are filmed, the two coaches usually fight at a UFC event. Lesnar declined the offer at first, but as he thought more about it he realized he could benefit from the fight. So he changed his mind and agreed to coach. "It's an opportunity for me to get my title back sooner rather than later," he said. "When I beat dos Santos, I get a rematch with Velasquez, and then I get my belt back. That's how I'm looking at it."

After filming a few episodes of the show, the contestants were impressed by Lesnar. "Honestly, at first when I heard Brock was coaching, I was like, 'I don't want to be on that guy's team. Go back to the WWE,' " one fighter said. "No disrespect, but that's what I first thought. But after meeting with him and his coaches, I'm real excited." Even dos Santos was surprised. "He's a pretty nice guy," dos Santos said.

In the reality show, coaches are encouraged to talk smack in order to attract more viewers to the program and to the pay-per-view fight to come. Lesnar refused to participate in such antics. He explained:

> I don't have to go around playing pranks and stirring up rivalries. These other fighters have to do that stuff because no one will watch it otherwise. I don't need a storyline. I'm Brock Lesnar, and people want to see me fight.

However, Lesnar's fighting would have to wait after he learned the diverticulitis returned again in May 2011. It wasn't nearly as serious as the first incident, but his training was cut short and his match with dos Santos was postponed. Lesnar said:

> Diverticulitis is an illness that never goes away. It's something that I've dealt with since my first occurrence and have been battling with it. I've been able to maintain it to a point where it's tolerable. There's a solution to every problem. I just gotta find the right solution to fix this problem. I love this sport, and I love what I do.

With a body seemingly cut from granite mixed with a white-hot temper, watching Lesnar fight is a true spectacle for millions of fans. White expects "The Baddest Dude on the Planet" to be a heavyweight force for years to come. "I consider Brock one of the best of all time, and he's just getting started," says White.

However, while Lesnar's popularity has never been higher, he truly doesn't care about being in the spotlight. In fact, while he understands the value of publicity to promote his sport, he would be happy if he never did another interview. Said Lesnar:

> It's very basic for me: train, sleep, family, fight. It's my life. I've been in front of the cameras for 10 or 12 years. I just don't put myself out there to the fans and (show) my private life to everybody. In today's day and age, with the Internet and cameras and cell phones, I just like being old school and living in the woods and living my life. I came from nothing. And at any moment, you can go back to having nothing.

Brock Lesnar in March 2011

TIMELINE

1977   Born July 12 in Webster, South Dakota.

1982   Starts wrestling competitively at age five.

1991   Joins Webster High School varsity wrestling team as
                a seventh-grader.

1994   Joins National Guard for brief stint.

1998   Wins the NJCAA national wrestling title.

2000   Wins the NCAA national heavyweight title; joins WWF.

2002   Makes WWF debut; becomes youngest WWE heavy-
                weight champion at age twenty-five.

2004   Tries out for Minnesota Vikings.

2007   Wins first mixed martial arts bout.

2008   Wins UFC heavyweight title in fourth professional
                mixed martial arts bout.

2009-10   After overcoming illness, defends UFC title twice.

SOURCES

Chapter One: Life on a Farm

p. 12,   "They never had . . ." Myron P. Medcalf, "UFC's Lesnar: Rage in the Ring, a Quiet Life Outside of It," *Minneapolis Star Tribune*, July 9, 2009.

p. 12,   "I don't (complain) . . ." Jim Schmaltz, "Brock and Roll: He Grew Up on a Farm, Baling Hay and Reading FLEX, but Now WWE Superstar Brock Lesnar Inflicts Pain on Other Humans for a Living. He's OK with That," *Flex*, February 2004.

p. 12,   "I pretty much . . ." "Brock on Hunting,"*Outdoor Life*, May 2009.

p. 14,   "From a really . . ." Joel Rippel, *Brock Lesnar: The Making of a Hard-Core Legend* (Chicago, Ill: Triumph Books, 2010), 7-8.

p. 14,   "Let's say you . . ." Dave Campbell, "The Ultimate Challenge," *Hamilton* (Ontario) *Spectator*, January 30, 2008.

p. 15,   "Admit it, accept . . ." Brock Lesnar and Paul Heyman, *Death Clutch: My Story of Determination, Domination, and Survival* (New York: William Morrow, 2011), 4.

p. 15,   "There's another match . . ." Ibid.

p. 15,   "Good job, Brock . . ." Ibid., 5.

p. 15,   "At a very . . ." Ibid., 6.

p. 16,   "He was always . . ." Rippel, *Brock Lesnar: The Making of a Hard-Core Legend*, 11.

p. 17,   "I wondered if . . ." Ibid., 14.

pp. 17-18, "Brock had his . . ." Ibid., 15.

pp. 18-19, "I developed the . . ." Lesnar and Heyman, *Death Clutch: My Story of Determination, Domination, and Survival*, 11.

pp. 20-21, "I was 17 years . . ." Schmaltz, "Brock and Roll: He Grew Up on a Farm, Baling Hay and Reading *FLEX*, but Now WWE Superstar Brock Lesnar Inflicts Pain on Other Humans for a Living. He's OK with That."

p. 22,   "Lucky for me," Lesnar and Heyman, *Death Clutch: My Story of Determination, Domination, and Survival*, 10.

Chapter Two: College Champion

p. 28,   "The loss to . . ." Lesnar and Heyman, *Death Clutch: My Story of Determination, Domination, and Survival*, 14.

p. 28,   "I'm going to . . ." Rippel, *Brock Lesnar: The Making of a Hard-Core Legend*, 44.

p. 29,   "Those are the . . ." Ibid., 46.

pp. 29-30, "I asked him . . ." Ibid., 50.

p. 33, "I am either . . ." Lesnar and Heyman, *Death Clutch: My Story of Determination, Domination, and Survival*, 25.

p. 34, "Better to lose . . ." Rippel, *Brock Lesnar: The Making of a Hard-Core Legend*, 58.

p. 35, "It was good . . ." Ibid.

p. 35, "When my hand . . ." Ibid., 59.

p. 36, "I never felt . . ." Ibid., 60.

p. 39, "I was being offered . . ." Lesnar and Heyman, *Death Clutch: My Story of Determination, Domination, and Survival*, 34.

Chapter Three: Get In to Get Out

p. 41, "Get in to . . ." Lesnar and Heyman, *Death Clutch: My Story of Determination, Domination, and Survival*, 45.

p. 42, "It was strange . . ." Rippel, *Brock Lesnar: The Making of a Hard-Core Legend*, 76-7.

p. 44, "Life on the . . ." Lesnar and Heyman, *Death Clutch: My Story of Determination, Domination, and Survival*, 57.

p. 46, "It wasn't about . . ." Ibid., 65.

p. 46, "It wasn't the . . ." John L. Wertheim, "Brock Lesnar," *Sports Illustrated*, March 30, 2009.

p. 46, "He's one of the best . . ." Rippel, *Brock Lesnar: The Making of a Hard-Core Legend*, 90.

p. 49, "and that's when . . ." Lesnar and Heyman, *Death Clutch: My Story of Determination, Domination, and Survival*, 95.

p. 49, "It was gratifying . . ." Greg Merritt, "Keeping it Real," *Muscle & Fitness*, February 2008.

p. 51, "This is no . . ." Tyrone Black, "Brock Lesnar Makes Name for Himself in MMA," Gambling911.com, June, 3, 2007, http://www.gambling911.com/Bruce-Lesnar-MMA-060307.html.

p. 51, "We've started with . . ." Scott Taylor, "Greenhorn Lesnar Needs Extra Work to Wear Purple, *Winnipeg Free Press*, August 7, 2004.

p. 52, "When we signed . . ." Scott Taylor, "Are Next Big Thing's Days Numbered?" *Winnipeg Free Press*, August 28, 2004.

p. 52, "In the business . . ." Rippel, *Brock Lesnar: The Making of a Hard-Core Legend*, 114.

p. 52, "Brock needs to . . ." Ibid.

pp. 52-53, "it would cause . . ." Ibid.

Chapter Four: Proving Ground

p. 57,   "He's stubborn . . ." Wertheim, "Brock Lesnar."

p. 57,   "He has tons . . ." Ibid.

pp. 60-61, "I would have . . ." Merritt, "Keeping it Real."

p. 61,   "I'm in this . . ." Ibid.

p. 62,   "That show was . . ." Jonathan Strickland, "How the Ultimate Fighting ChampionshipWorks," How Stuff Works, http://entertainment.howstuffworks.com/ufc4.htm.

p. 64,   "There are some . . ." Rippel, *Brock Lesnar: The Making of a Hard-Core Legend*, 129.

p. 66,   "Lesnar was bigger . . ." Jonathan Snowden and Kendall Shields, *The MMA Encyclopedia* (Toronto, Canada: ECW Press, 2010), 250.

p. 66,   "The question surrounding . . ." "Maybe Next Time, Brock," *Hamilton* (Ontario) *Spectator*, February 4, 2008.

p. 66,   "Man versus beast . . ." Rippel, *Brock Lesnar: The Making of a Hard-Core Legend*, 132.

p. 67,   "That referee . . ." Ibid.

p. 67,   "I'm still disgusted . . ." Ibid., 133.

Chapter Five: Can You See Me Now?

p. 69,   "The people that . . ." Wertheim, "Brock Lesnar."

p. 73,   "I fell off . . ." Loretta Hunt, "Lesnar Shuts Down Herring," Sherdog.com, August 10, 2008, http://www.sherdog.com/news/articles/Lesnar-Shuts-Down-Herring-13979.

p. 73,   "Can you see . . ." Ibid.

p. 74,   "I'm getting sick . . ." Rippel, *Brock Lesnar: The Making of a Hard-Core Legend*, 136.

p. 74,   "Honest to God . . ." Brian Knapp, "Lesnar Punch Blindsided Couture," Sherdog.com, http://www.sherdog.com/news/articles/Lesnar-Punch-Blindsided-Couture-15185.

p. 76,   "Right away, it . . ." Ibid.

p. 76,   "Honestly, I didn't . . ." Ibid.

p. 76,   "I can't believe it . . ." Joe Hall, "Lesnar Takes Couture's Title, Sherdog.com http://www.sherdog.com/news/articles/Lesnar-Takes-Coutures-Title-15178.

p. 77,   "Guys aren't just . . ." John L. Wertheim, "The Haute Couture," *Sports Illustrated*, November 24, 2008, 18.

p. 77,   "You've got my . . ." Ibid.

p. 78,   "Brock Lesnar has . . ." "Lesnar to Battle Mir," *Guelph* (Ontario) *Mercury*, March 3, 2009.

p. 78,   "He's fought for . . ." Neil Davidson, "Battle of the Big Boys," *Hamilton* (Ontario) *Spectator*, July 11, 2009.

p. 79,   "Obviously, Brock then . . ." Ibid.

p. 82,   "I love it . . ." Bernard Fernandez, "Brock Lesnar a Sore Winner in UFC Bout with Mir," *Philadelphia Daily News*, July 12, 2009.

p. 82,   "Brock went so far . . ." Ibid.

p. 83,   "I'm a sore . . ." Ibid.

Chapter Six: Near-Death and Back

p. 85,   "I don't know . . ." Adam Hill, "Lesnar's Actions Disgust Couture," *Las Vegas Review-Journal*, July 16, 2009.

p. 85,   "Those that do . . ." Rippel, *Brock Lesnar: The Making of a Hard-Core Legend*, 146-7.

p. 88,   "This guy is . . ." Ibid., 148-9.

p. 88,   "lame," Ibid, 150.

p. 88,   "He may be . . ." Ibid.

p. 89,   "He said he's . . ." Ibid., 153.

p. 92,   "He's in rough . . ." "Lesnar 'In Really Bad Shape' in Hospital," *Toronto Star*, November 15, 2009.

p. 92,   "The world's baddest . . ." Lesnar and Heyman, *Death Clutch: My Story of Determination, Domination, and Survival*, 195.

p. 94,   "If I touch . . ." Myron P. Medcalf, "Man of the Hour," *Minneapolis Star Tribune*, July 3, 2010.

p. 94,   "I could have just . . ." Adam Hill, "Off 'Deathbed,' Lesnar Gives Serenity a Try," *Las Vegas Review-Journal*, July 2, 2010.

p. 96,   "I just had to . . ." Adam Hill, "Lesnar Overcomes First-Round Onslaught, Hands Carwin First Defeat," *Las Vegas Review-Journal*, July 4, 2010.

p. 96,   "This is about . . ." Ibid.

p. 97,   "I knew there . . ." Jamie Pandaram, "Lesnar Defeat Leaves Mark of Cain Velasquez on Mexican Fighting Record," *Sydney Morning Herald*, October 25, 2010.

p. 97,   "It's an opportunity . . ." Case Keefer, "Brock Lesnar Tries to Enjoy Experience; Sees Opportunity in 'The Ultimate Fighter,'" *Las Vegas Sun*, January 26, 2011.

p. 97,   "Honestly, at first . . ." Ibid.

p. 97,   "He's a pretty . . ." Ibid.

p. 98,   "I don't have to . . ." Ibid.

p. 98,   "Diverticulitis is an . . ." Thomas Gerbasi, "Lesnar Out, Dos Santos to Face Carwin," ufc.com, http://www.ufc.com/news/Lesnar-Out-of-UFC-131-Carwin-to-face-dos-Santos.

pp. 98-99, "I consider Brock . . ." Kevin Iole, "Lesnar Separates Public From Private," YahooSports.com, October 22, 2010, http://sports.yahoo.com/mma/news?slug=ki-lesnar102210.

p. 99,   "It's very basic . . ." Ibid.

BIBLIOGRAPHY

Black, Tyrone. "Brock Lesnar Makes Name for Himself in MMA." Gambling911.com, June 3, 2007. http://www.gambling911.com/Bruce-Lesnar-MMA-060307.html.

Campbell, Dave. "The Ultimate Challenge." *Hamilton* (Ontario) *Spectator*, January 30, 2008.

Canadian Press. "Lesnar Team Shows its Mettle on Season 13 of 'The Ultimate Fighter.'" March 29, 2011.

Davidson, Neil. "Battle of the Big Boys." *Hamilton* (Ontario) *Spectator*, July 11, 2009.

Fernandez, Bernard. "Brock Lesnar a Sore Winner in UFC Bout with Mir." *Philadelphia Daily News*, July 12, 2009.

Guelph (Ontario) *Mercury*. "Lesnar to Battle Mir." March 3, 2009.

Hall, Joe. "Lesnar Takes Couture's Title." Sherdog.com, November 16, 2008. http://www.sherdog.com/news/articles/Lesnar-Takes-Coutures-Title-15178.

Hamilton (Ontario) *Spectator*. "Maybe Next Time, Brock." February 4, 2008.

Hill, Adam. "Lesnar's Actions Disgust Couture" *Las Vegas Review-Journal*, July 16, 2009.

———. "Off 'Deathbed,' Lesnar Gives Serenity a Try." *Las Vegas Review-Journal*, July 2, 2010.

———. "Lesnar Overcomes First-Round Onslaught, Hands Carwin First Defeat." *Las Vegas Review-Journal*, July 4, 2010.

Hunt, Loretta. "Lesnar Shuts Down Herring." Sherdog.com, August 10, 2008. http://www.sherdog.com/news/articles/Lesnar-Shuts-Down-Herring-13979.

Iole, Kevin. "Lesnar Separates Public From Private." YahooSports.com, October 22, 2010. http://sports.yahoo.com/mma/news?slug=ki-lesnar102210.

Keefer, Case. "Brock Lesnar Tries to Enjoy Experience; Sees Opportunity in 'The Ultimate Fighter.'" *Las Vegas Sun*, January 26, 2011.

Knapp, Brian. "Lesnar Punch Blindsided Couture." Sherdog.com, November 17, 2008. http://www.sherdog.com/news/articles/Lesnar-Punch-Blindsided-Couture-15185.

Lesnar, Brock, and Paul Heyman. *Death Clutch: My Story of Determination, Domination, and Survival*. New York: William Morrow, 2011.

McMahon, Vince. Brock Lesnar: *Here Comes the Pain!* DVD, World Wrestling Entertainment, Inc., 2003.

Medcalf, Myron P. "Man of the Hour." *Minneapolis Star Tribune*, July 3, 2010.

———. "UFC's Lesnar: Rage in the Ring, a Quiet Life Outside of It." *Minneapolis Star Tribune*, July 9, 2009.

Merritt, Greg. "Keeping it Real." *Muscle & Fitness*, February 2008.

Outdoor Life. "Brock Lesnar."May 2009.

Rippel, Joel. *Brock Lesnar: The Making of a Hard-Core Legend*. Chicago, Ill: Triumph Books, 2010.

Schmaltz, Jim. "Brock and Roll." *Flex*, February 2004.

Snowden, Jonathan, and Kendall Shields. *The MMA Encyclopedia*, Toronto, Canada: ECW Press, 2010.

Toronto Star. "Lesnar 'In Really Bad Shape' in Hospital." November 15, 2009.

Strickland, Jonathan. "How the Ultimate Fighting Championship Works." *How Stuff Works*, http://entertainment.howstuffworks.com/ufc4.htm.

Taylor, Scott. "Greenhorn Lesnar Needs Extra Work to Wear Purple." *Winnipeg Free Press*, August 7, 2004.

———. "Are Next Big Thing's Days Numbered?" *Winnipeg Free Press*, August 28, 2004.

Wertheim, John L. "Brock Lesnar." *Sports Illustrated*, March 30, 2009.

WEB SITES

http://www.deathclutch.com

> Brock Lesnar's official site. It includes his biography, photos, recent news about him, and information about his Death Clutch clothing line, including an online store.

http://www.ufc.com

> The Ultimate Fighting Championship official site. It includes upcoming events, results of all UFC fights, overviews of fighters, information on training camps, and the latest news in the UFC.

http://mixedmartialarts.com

> This Web site provides information such as event results and statistics, fight videos, and extensive training videos focusing techniques and conditioning.

INDEX

New Japan Pro Wrestling, 52-54, 60
NJCAA championships (National Junior College Athletic Association), 27, 29
Nogueira, Antonio, 77

Olsen, David, 38, 52
OVW (Ohio Valley Wrestling), 42

Panagos, Jim, 51
Paulson, Erik, 70
pay-per-view events, 11, 46, 53, 62-63, 65, 70, 79, 82, 97
pro wrestling, 42, 44

RAW wrestling, 44
Rheingans, Brad, 41
Richesson, Luke, 93
Robinson, J., 29-31, 38
Rogan, Joe, 82
Ross, Jim, 85

Schiley, John, 12, 16-17, 24, 35
SEG (Semaphore Entertain Group), 62-63
Shamrock, Ken, 62-63
SummerSlam, 45

Tampa Bay Buchaneers, 36-38
Tice, Mike, 51
TNA (Total Nonstop Action Wrestling), 54-55
TUF (The Ultimate Fighter), 63, 97

UFC (Ultimate Fighting Championship), 70-71, 74, 82
    about the sport, 86-87, *86*
    history, 60, 62-63
University of Minnesota, 29-31, 34

Velasquez, Cain, 96-97

Welch, Peter, 70, 93
White, Dana, 60, 62-63, 66, 82, 88-89, 92, *92,* 97-99
Wiley, Mike, 27
Wrestlemania, 48-49
WWE (World Wrestling Entertainment), 38, 44-45, 48, 52-53, 54-55, 71, 82
WWF (World Wrestling Federation), 38, 42-44

Yamasaki, Mario, 76

PHOTO CREDITS